Type/Variant House

Vincent James

Edited by Oscar Riera Ojeda

Introduction by Thomas Fisher

First published in the
United States of America by:
Rockport Publishers, Inc.
33 Commercial Street
Gloucester, Massachusetts 01930-5089
Telephone: (978) 282-9590
Facsimile: (978) 283-2742

Distributed to the book trade
and art trade in the United States by:
North Light Books, an imprint of
F & W Publications
1507 Dana Avenue
Cincinnati, Ohio 45207
Telephone: (800) 289-0963

Other Distribution by:
Rockport Publishers, Inc.
Gloucester, Massachusetts 01930-5089

ISBN 1-56496-523-6

10 9 8 7 6 5 4 3 2 1

contents

(re)Visiting the Machine in the Garden

by Thomas Fisher

Across fields plowed into variegated patterns, past farm sheds wrapped in rusting metal, down a logging road threaded through a deciduous forest, you come upon this house, suddenly, as if it were forgotten in the woods. Looking, at first, like an old ore dock by the lake, a common sight north of here, the Type/Variant House, as architect Vincent James calls it, seems dislocated in time as well as in space. Its façade, composed of stacked, nearly windowless volumes wrapped in oxidizing copper, appears modern and antiquated, robust and ruinous, all at once. ▮ That first impression fades as you enter and move through what is, in fact, an elegant and eminently livable 8,000-square-foot house. Yet first impressions shouldn't be ignored. The sense of this house as a remnant of technology set in untrammeled nature brings to mind the metaphor of *The Machine in the Garden,* the 1964 book by historian Leo Marx. Marx argued there that the juxtaposition of early industry and the American wilderness, which figured so prominently in the writing of nineteenth-century authors such as Henry David Thoreau and Nathaniel Hawthorne, represented a confrontation between two of our culture's most powerful myths: our technological know-how and our Edenic landscape. That confrontation has played itself out in various ways in American culture, but rarely in architecture with as much subtlety as the Type/Variant House. ▮ Most modernist architects have taken a more literal approach to the question of technology and nature. When Le Corbusier, in the early twentieth century, envisioned sleek towers or ship-like houses standing in a park or an otherwise bucolic setting, the issue seemed clear: the building as a "machine for living in" stood clearly defined and different from the nature around it. By the end of the century, however, the issue seems much less clear.

Isn't technology, as a human construct, also an extension of nature or at least of human nature? And hasn't nature become so affected by human activities that it is now almost an extension of technology? The Type/Variant House raises these and other related questions, demonstrating a conceptual strength that matches its visual presence. The structure may appear isolated on its 200 acres of woods and lake where one of the owners spent part of her childhood, but this is a work of architecture near the center of current thinking.   ∎ 1 For most of this century and the last, we have conceived of machines as predictable, automatic, and universal devices that relieve us of labor. The notion of architecture as a kind of machine embraced the same idea: modernist buildings not only began to look like machines—uniform, repetitive, and made of steel—but they sought to act like one, providing a flow of space and ease of maintenance that would, in theory at least, reduce our labor. To be sure, various architects had different notions of how to accomplish that: Ludwig Mies van der Rohe emphasized a reduction of physical obstacles, while Marcel Breuer focused on the prefabrication of elements. But few questioned the idea of a machine. ∎ By the late twentieth century, our conception of the machine has become more nuanced. With ample evidence of the machine's power to pollute and destroy, we clearly have less optimism about its universal benefits. We also have begun to realize that the machine extends beyond the object we label as such to the social and technological systems that surround it. And it is these systems that have shown us how machines can be adaptive and hybrid: self-correcting computer-controlled production systems, for example, or heterogeneous, decentralized information systems such as the Internet. ∎

The Type/Variant House has this hybrid machine-like quality. It recalls, for example, the work of several modernist architects, some of them rarely mentioned in the same breath. The house, however, is not an eclectic assembly of visual quotations, so typical of Postmodern architecture, but a system of architectural elements that is consistent and yet highly adaptive to its setting. ▮ The tall, glazed, pavilion-like living and dining room, which brings to mind some of the houses of Mies van der Rohe and early Philip Johnson, continues the visual sweep of the forest down the hill and out to the adjacent lake. The up-ended guest-room boxes, whose idiosyncratic cut-outs and uncertain scale recall John Hejduk's houses and sculptures, elevate you into the surrounding trees. The horizontal boxes, with their strip windows and cantilevers echoing the early work of Marcel Breuer, give sliced vistas of the ground, the foliage, and the water. Meanwhile, the intersecting glass-ended enclosures, reminiscent of the overlapping spaces in some of Paul Rudolph's houses from the 1960s, make you feel as if you are being propelled into the landscape, your view shot down a tube of space and far out across the lake or along the shore. ▮ ll If the house shows how our idea of the machine has become more complex and adaptive, so too does it reveal nuances in the relationship of technology and nature. Marx's book, like many of the nineteenth-century writers he referred to, assumed that the machine stood in the garden, and that technology might affect nature but rarely the other way around. The Type/Variant House suggests otherwise, showing how nature can overcome the most sophisticated technology. The house's copper cladding, once mined out of the earth, will eventually return to it: visually, it will turn the color of the area's rich black soil and then

15

the vibrant green of the forest, and physically, the copper will oxidize and send its surface, ever so slowly, back to where it came from. ▮ The house also demonstrates how the garden can exist inside the machine. Horizontal layers of Douglas fir cover the floor, walls, and ceilings of most of the house, clear-coated to retain the color of the wood the day it was cut. As a result, the interior of the house recalls both a rustic cabin and a lumber yard, with wood stacked all around you like preserved specimens of the living trees outside the windows. This garden inside the machine may be a symbolic one, frozen in time and altered in state, but it is a kind of nature nonetheless. ▮ Finally, the house indicates how we sometimes use the machine to replicate nature. An example of this is the living room fireplace, one of the most impressive structures of its kind in recent architecture. Freestanding and backlit by clerestory windows, the fireplace consists of thin layers of slate, stacked horizontally to the full height of the living room. This modern megalith creates an artificial stratification more perfect—and so more sublime—than a real cliff, with a fire like the earth's molten core within it.   ▮ lll But what is this nature we try so hard to relate to? Is it always what it seems? The owners' ethnographic collections include objects ranging from ceremonial masks to antique varsity team photographs which are usually displayed in rows or grids that bring out the subtle variations among similar things. This collector sensibility recalls the early naturalists, out in nature, gathering and categorizing what they find, except that what the owners of this house assemble are what others have made, things not of nature so much as of human nature. ▮ That blurring of the natural and artificial, in turn, suggests that the machine and the garden

have begun to merge, that the products of technology have become a kind of second nature for us just as the products of

nature increasingly have a technology—genetic engineering—driving them. You sense this merging in the house. James designed

it with the owners' collections in mind: he focused on a type—a copper-clad, wood-lined tube of space—and then played

variations on the theme: elevating the box, cantilevering it, up-ending it, cutting the corners out of it, setting one inside

another, turning one's back to the others, and so on. The copper boxes thus begin to take on the character of natural objects,

their forms as diverse and their surfaces as weathered as the trees around them. ▮ A similar merging of technology and nature

occurs inside. The house has entire walls of glass, some of which swing out or fold back, making you feel as if you are a part

of the forest around you, a reminder of how we use technology to reconnect us to nature and, by implication, to ourselves.

That drive to reconnect to nature, to understand it, penetrate it, not only underlies much modern architecture, but much of

modern science and art as well. ▮ The Type/Variant House is a masterful exploration of form, space, and material. Its

lasting power, however, lies in its revisiting a metaphor whose value was long thought exhausted. Not only is the notion of

the machine in the garden much more complex and more interesting than the original conception of the idea, but, as Vincent

James shows in this house, we have only begun to explore its meaning.

Thomas Fisher ▮ Minneapolis, Minnesota ▮ October 31, 1997

Thomas Fisher, dean of the College of Architecture and Landscape Architecture at the University of Minnesota, served on the editorial staff of *Progressive Architecture* magazine for nearly fourteen years, first as the technics editor and later as the executive editor and editorial director. He also served as the editorial director of *Building Renovation* magazine. Educated at Cornell University in architecture and Case Western Reserve University in intellectual history, he came to those editorial positions having worked in architectural offices as a designer and project manager and in state government as a historical architect and a regional preservation officer. The focus of his work has been on architecture as a cultural phenomena and on architecture as culture.

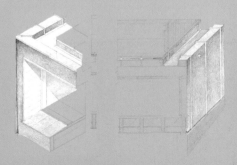

by Vincent James

The Type/Variant House is the second of three residential projects I designed between 1990 and 1997. With the Anderson Residence, to be located on Lake Superior and as yet unbuilt, I began to explore a set of ideas that would culminate in the Type/Variant House. Frustrated by the overburdened symbolic and formal agenda of American architecture in the 1980s, I became intrigued by the rural industrial structures of the Upper Midwest. Although generally not considered architecture, these ore docks, granaries and bridges seemed to possess a simple integrity in their blunt forms and explicit tectonics. Like the natural environment they are symbolically mute, free from any intended meaning beyond the direct expression of their function. ▌ In the Anderson Residence I did not see the program as an abstract generator of form, but as activity given particular meaning by its context—in this case the powerful Lake Superior environment. In this sense the relationship of program to site became clear as primary architectural content, preceding the formal development of the project. Drawings of the Anderson Residence, like the watercolors "Axis of Domestic Rituals" and "Heated Pool," prefigured many of the ideas that would later be realized in the Type/Variant House. ▌ The Dayton Residence in Minneapolis, designed after the other two houses and completed in 1997, explores similar issues of site and program but from a different perspective. If the Type/Variant House and Anderson Residence could be described as country houses, the Dayton Residence is a city house. Here the context is not natural but cultural. The play between the interior and exterior takes on significance as the strictly modern, almost laconic, design is placed within a residential context of sentimental eclecticism. ▌ **Type/Variant House** Located on a large lake in

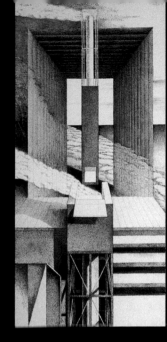

Anderson Residence, watercolor perspectives and model

northern Wisconsin, the Type/Variant House is approached from the west along a gravel road which follows an abandoned logging trail. As the road descends into a ravine, the house comes into view as an enigmatic assembly of copper forms, veiled by the forest. From this vantage point it can be simultaneously understood as a sculptural whole and as an ensemble of cubic volumes defining a variety of exterior spaces. After arriving in the entry court, the sequence through the house becomes episodic, a chain of experiences in which a sense of the whole is elusive, yet contained within the individual parts. ▮ In 1994, as we began to generate ideas for the house, the owners' fascination for what was termed the "type/variant" developed into the underpinning concept for the project. As in a butterfly collection, the play between the similarities and differences of objects in a collection is fundamental to its aesthetic appeal. The Type/Variant House was conceived as a "collection" of wood-framed, copper-clad volumes, each distinguished by its unique orientation, proportions and natural light. The rooms and spaces defined by the cubic volumes are oriented orthogonally to emphasize a series of specific views of the forest and the exterior of the house. ▮ The house was designed for a family of seven with accommodations for additional guests in two adjacent structures. The living area, which is centrally located under a large horizontal volume containing bedrooms, is anchored by a slate-clad fireplace. The fully glazed living and dining room is enclosed by a series of louvered screens that provide privacy and light control. Circulation links the three floors in a series of overlapping rectangles, some explicit and others implicit. It also connects the interior spaces to the courtyards and roof terraces. Stairs, ramps and bridges—the only diagonal elements

in the composition—are counterpoised against the rectilinear geometry of the house. ▊ **Materials** The naturally weath-

ering materials and simple details of the Type/Variant House were also inspired, in part, by the rural industrial structures of

the Upper Midwest which achieve an elegant clarity through the expediencies of construction. The resulting tectonics are both

familiar and abstract, compatible with the owners' desire for a rustic warmth that avoids sentimentality. ▊ The materials of

the house, primarily Douglas fir, copper and bluestone, are assembled in a variety of contrapuntal rhythms. The wood frame

structure establishes the two-foot module of the house and the dominant tectonic rhythm. The interior finishes include

exposed wood framing in the living areas and sleeping loft, with tongue-and-groove wood cladding in other areas of the

house. The wood "lining" is longitudinally oriented to emphasize the tube-like qualities of the interior spaces. ▊ The copper

siding was left to age naturally. At the completion of construction in October 1996, a range of patinas could be seen reflecting

the twelve-month installation period; the pink-orange of bright copper, an indigo blue and a deep purple-brown. The familiar

copper green will take years to develop. This natural process is considered by the owner to be one of the most important

aesthetic experiences of the house. As he comments, "the rain, snow and airborne impurities all leave their mark on its surface

as a reminder of how ephemeral most things are." ▊ A dialectic between the building's wood tectonics and the surrounding

forest is revealed by the copper cladding which mediates between the inner (preserved) and the outer (weathering) enviroments.

As the copper weathers into the natural setting, the contrast between the inside and outside is amplified. Similarly, the stone

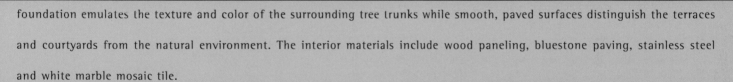

foundation emulates the texture and color of the surrounding tree trunks while smooth, paved surfaces distinguish the terraces and courtyards from the natural environment. The interior materials include wood paneling, bluestone paving, stainless steel and white marble mosaic tile.

Vincent James ▌ Minneapolis, Minnesota ▌ December 12, 1997

Type/Variant House

Drawings and Photographs

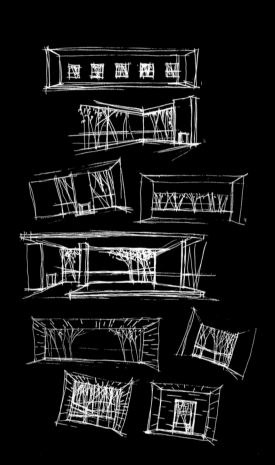

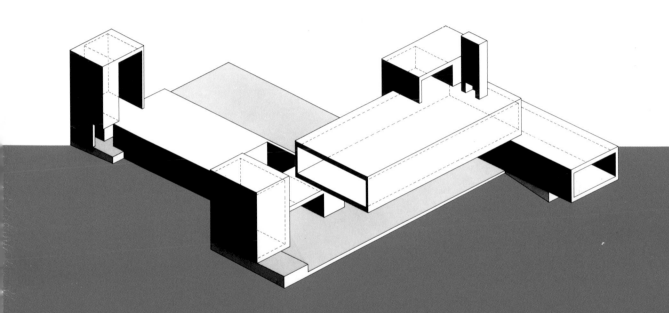

Site plan

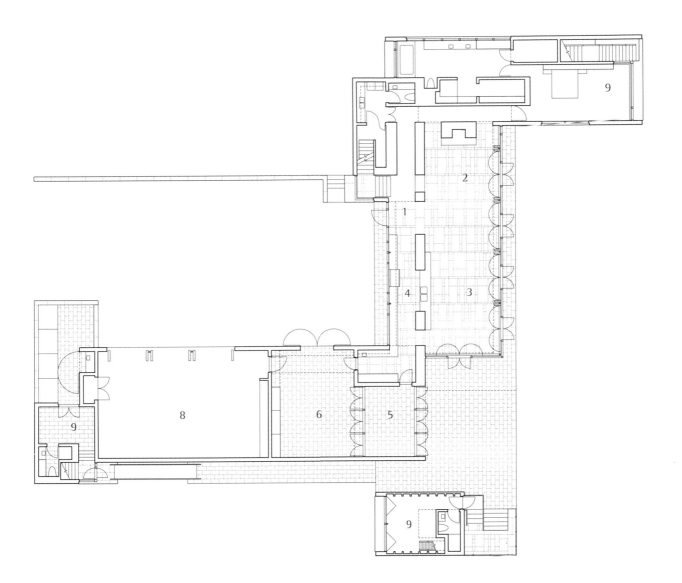

First floor plan

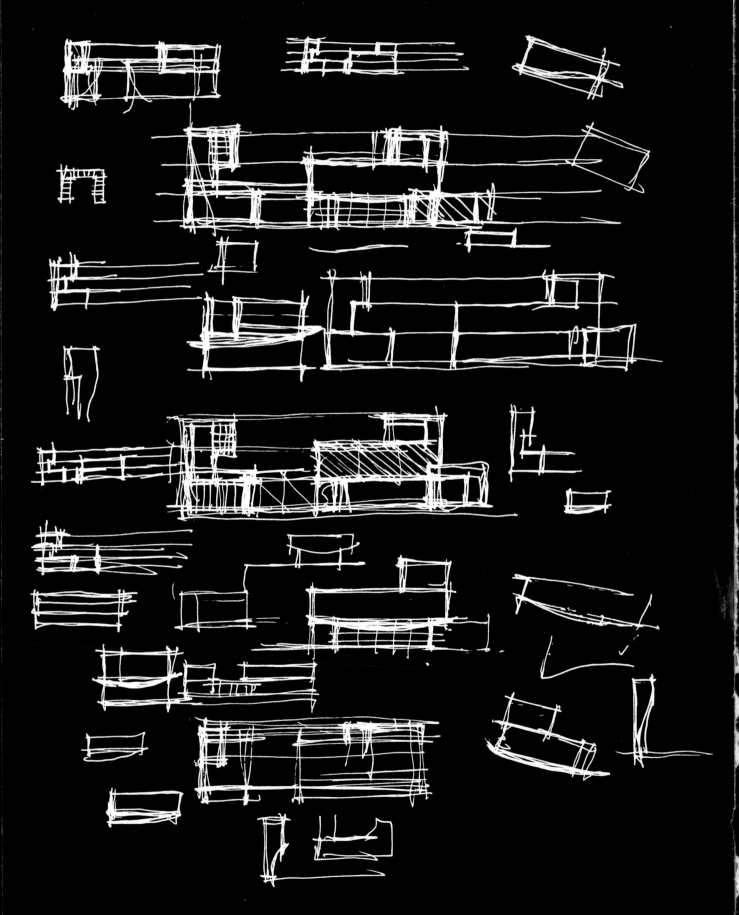

15 Detail of copper surfaces and early floor plan sketch (previous spread) Early interior perspective and elevation sketches (this spread) Volumetric study (foldout page)

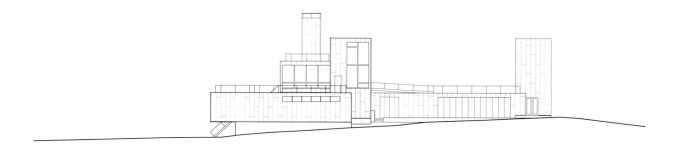

North elevation

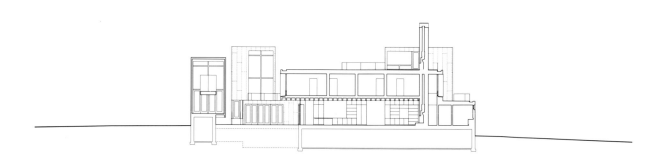

Longitudinal section looking west

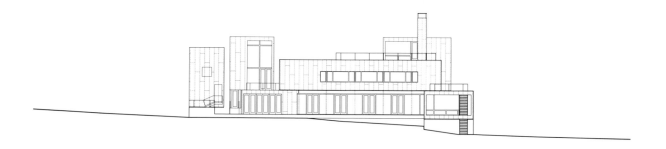

East elevation

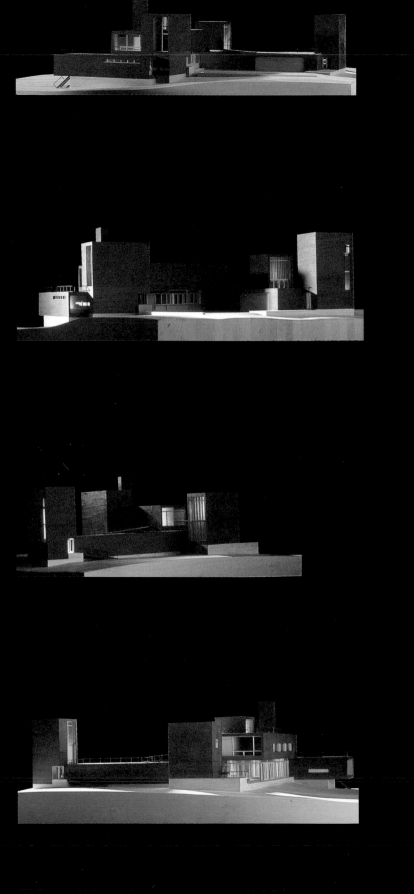

Wall section at living / bedroom

1   Copper sheathing
2   Furring
3   Copper skirt
4   Bluestone pavers
5   Bluestone facing
6   Poured concrete foundation
7   CMU foundation wall
8   Air supply duct
9   Folding privacy screen
10 Steel column
11 Wood window
12 Light shelf
13 Column stiffener
14 Butt-glazed transom glass
15 Recessed column bearing plate
16 Wood tongue-and-groove ceiling with battens
17 Concealed hanger for laminated wood beam
18 Wood veneered cabinet
19 Recess for inswing window
20 Wood tongue-and-groove wall
21 Perimeter gutter
22 Copper mesh guardrail

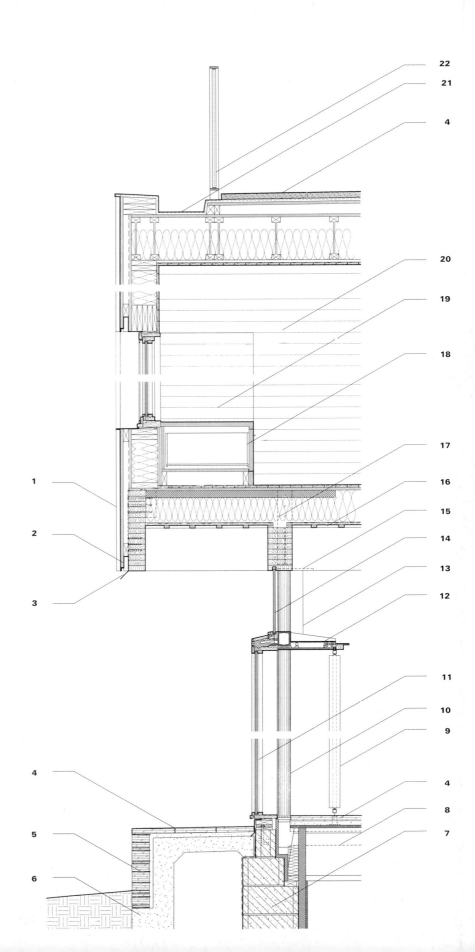

Construction process
(this, previous and following spreads)

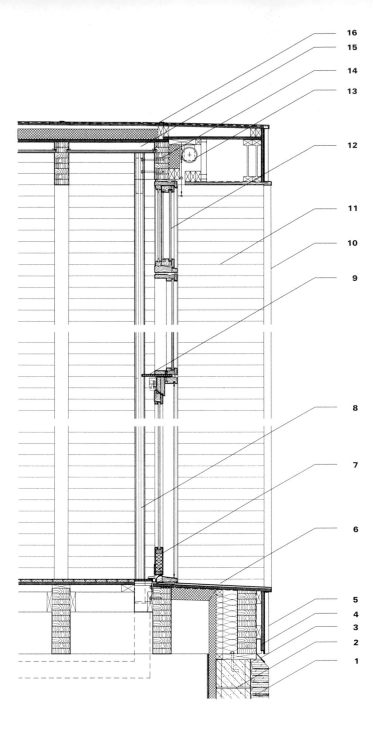
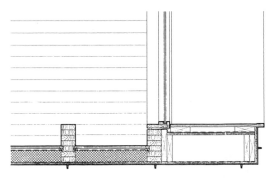

Plan and section at loft

1   Bluestone facing
2   CMU foundation wall
3   Copper skirt
4   Furring
5   Copper sheathing
6   Copper sill
7   Bifold doors
8   Steel column
9   Steel wind brace
10 Copper sheathing cap plate
11 Wood tongue-and-groove sheathing
12 Wood window
13 Concealed sun shade
14 Laminated wood beam
15 Rigid insulation
16 Soldered copper roof sheathing

21 22 23 24 25 26 Entry court from driveway during winter (previous spread) Detail at entry (left) View of entry court from tower (top) View of tower from entry court (middle) View of entry court looking south (bottom) View from courtyard toward entry (following spread)

27 28 29 Courtyard from entry court (previous and this spread) Courtyard (right)

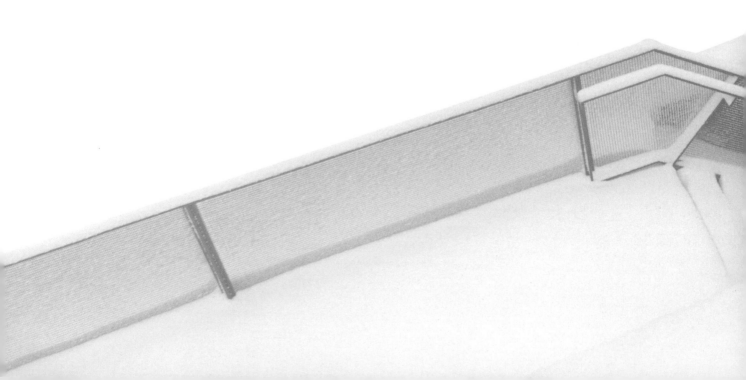

40 41 42 43 Partial east view (previous spread) East view from lake (left) Stair into mystery object (above) View north to master bedroom (following spread)

44 45 46 47 48 Detail of copper and bluestone wall (previous spread) Detail of tower ramp landing (left) Southwest view of tower and mystery object (top) South view of tower (middle) Southwest view of mystery object (bottom)

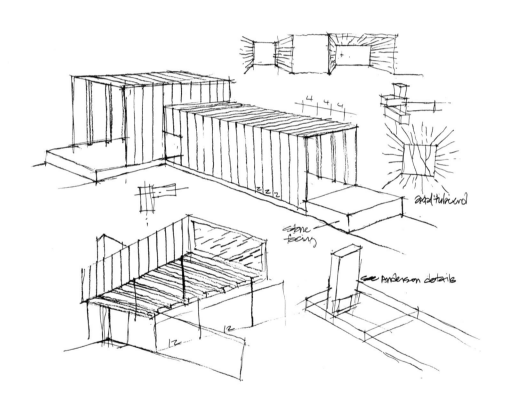

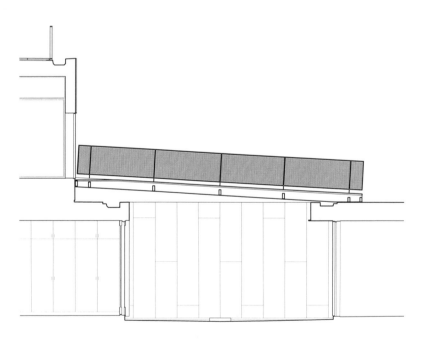

Section at courtyard and bridge (above) View of door into second floor from bridge (right)

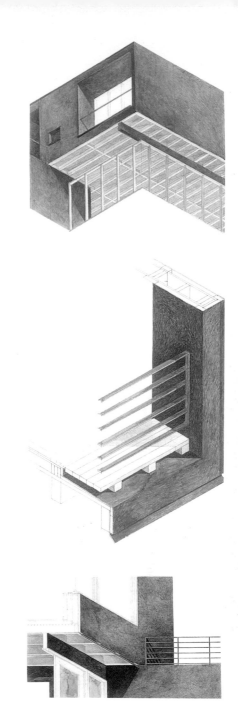

55 View of tower from roof terrace (left)
Watercolor sketches (above)

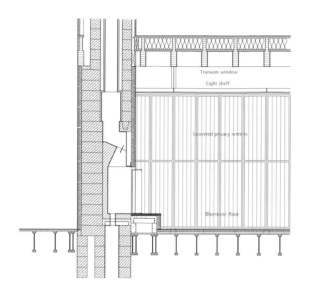

Transom window

Light shelf

Louvered privacy screens

Bluestone floor

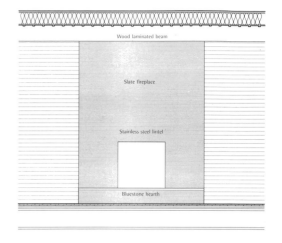

Wood laminated beam

Slate fireplace

Stainless steel lintel

Bluestone hearth

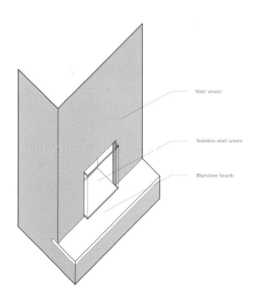

Slate veneer

Stainless steel screen

Bluestone hearth

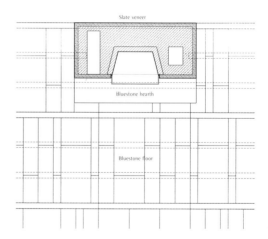

Slate veneer

Bluestone hearth

Bluestone floor

Fireplace in section (upper left) Elevation (upper right) Axonometric (lower left) Plan (lower right)

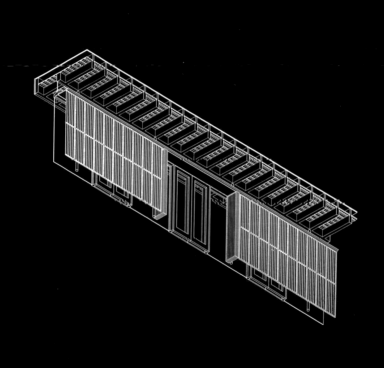

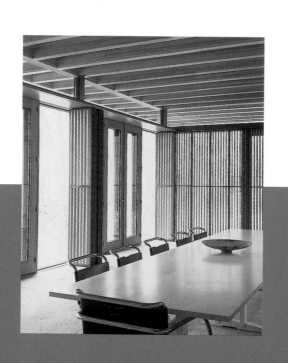

65 66 Master bedroom (top) Stair to third floor studio (following page)

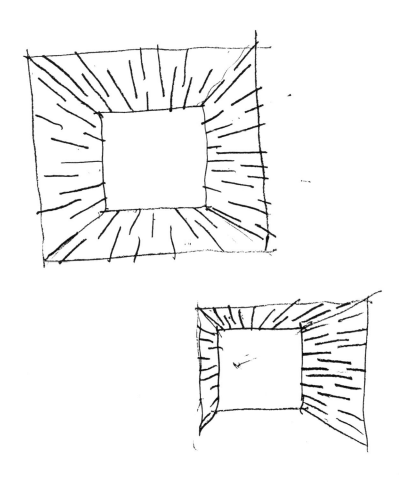

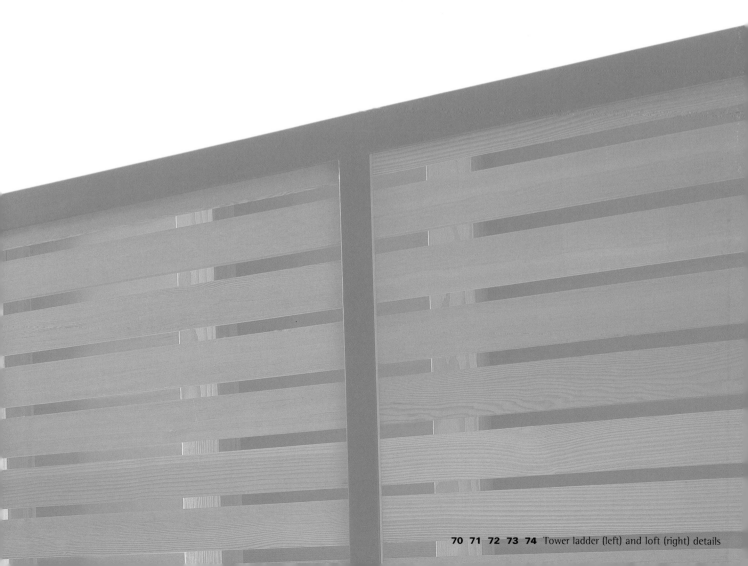

70 71 72 73 74 Tower ladder (left) and loft (right) details

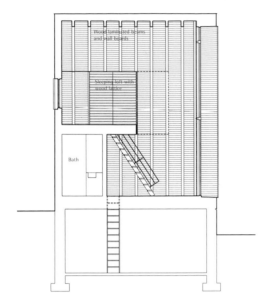

Wood laminated beams
and wall boards

Sleeping loft with
wood lattice

Bath

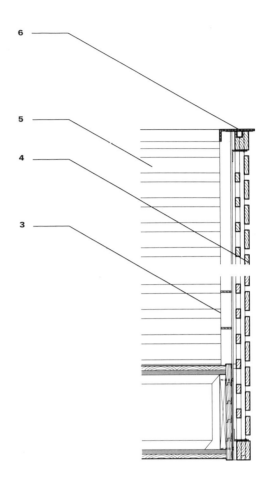

6

5

4

3

2

1

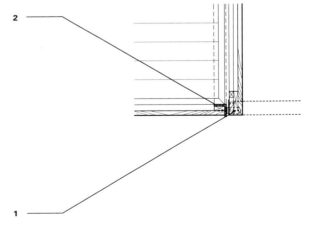

Mystery object section and details

1   Pivot hinge
2   Steel frame
3   Steel guardrail
4   Wood lattice door
5   Wood lattice
6   Steel top plate

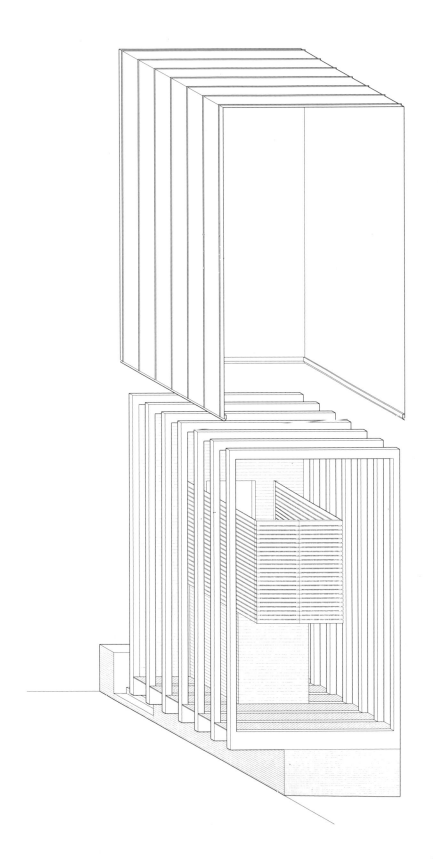

Detail of studio stair (previous foldout) Night view of rooftop fireplace (this spread)

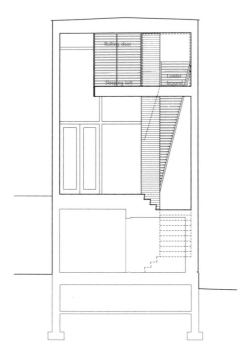

Tower section and details

1   Wood tongue-and-groove flooring

2   Wood enclosure ladder

3   Steel ladder

4   Wood tongue-and-groove sheathing

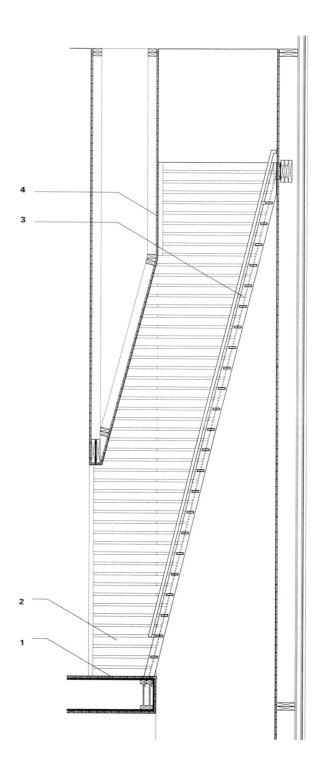

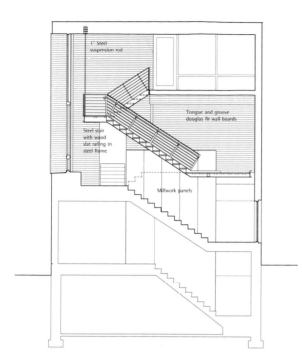

Legend on drawing:
- 1" Steel suspension rod
- Tongue and groove douglas fir wall boards
- Steel stair with wood slat railing in steel frame
- Millwork panels

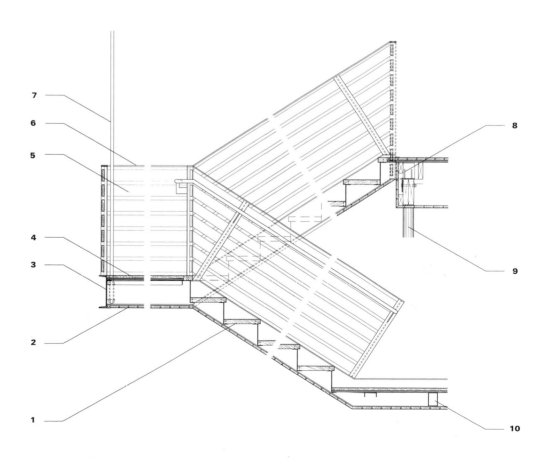

Project Name:	Type/Variant House
Owner:	Withheld at owners' request
Location:	Northern Wisconsin
Architect:	Vincent James Associates Inc.
	(project initiated by
	James/Snow Architects Inc.)

314 Clifton Avenue South
Minneapolis, Minnesota 55403
612-872-6370

National Honor Award, American Institute of Architects, 1998.
Honor Award, American Institute of Architects, Minnesota, 1996.

Design Team: Vincent James, principal in charge
Paul Yaggie, project architect
Nathan Knutson, Nancy Blankfard,
collaborators
Andrew Dull, Steve Lazen,
Krista Scheib, Julie Snow,
Taavo Somer, Kate Wyberg,
project team.

Consultants: Structural: The McSherry Group Inc.
Mechanical: Vogt Mechanical
Landscape: Coen + Stumpf
Associates, Inc.

General Contractor: Yerigan Construction Company

27741 University Avenue North
Isanti, Minnesota 55040
612-444-5353

Building Area: 8,000 square feet
Date of Design: 1994-1996
Date of Completion: Summer 1997

With the 1996 completion of the Type/Variant House and the recently completed Dayton Residence, Vincent James has emerged as or

the most interesting architects currently practicing in the Midwest. His residential projects seek to broaden the dialectical relatior

between building and site. Instead of maintaining the Modernist preoccupation with functional and aesthetic autonomy, his hc

acknowledge the many overlaps and juxtapositions between building and site that result in a complex intertwining of func

aesthetics and psychology. In so doing, the site, no longer characterized only as the physical context, is redefined to include

programmatic, material and cultural conditions of each project. ▮ Vincent James founded his practice in Minneapolis in 1

He received a master of architecture degree in 1978 from the University of Wisconsin/Milwaukee. Vincent has taught architecture a

University of Minnesota and the University of Wisconsin/Milwaukee. He was Favrot Visiting Chair in architecture at Tulane Unive

1998-1999. ▮ Vincent James Associates Inc., Architects is located in Minneapolis, Minnesota and currently employs a staff of

architects and designers. The firm's work includes museums, other cultural and institutional projects, and residences. The wo

Vincent James Associates has been recognized through recent design awards and publications.

Vincent James

About the Author

Originally from Buenos Aires, Oscar Riera Ojeda is an editor and designer who practices in the United States, South America and Europe from his office in Boston. He is vice-director of the Spanish-Argentinian magazine *Casas Internacional,* and is the creator of several series of architectural publications for Rockport Publishers in addition to the *Single Building* series, including *Ten Houses, Contemporary World Architects, Architecture in Detail* and *Art and Architecture.* Other architectural publications include the *New American* series for the Whitney Library of Design, as well as several monographs on the work of renowned architects.

The text was edited by Mark Denton, an architect practicing in Santa Monica, California and New London, Connecticut.

photographic credits